CONTENTS

Author Chris Oxlade

Why is summer warm and sunny?

The Earth is tipped to one side as it moves round the Sun. Some of the year, the north half of the Earth faces the Sun. Then the Sun is higher in the sky, making the weather warm. This is summer. When the southern half of the Earth faces the Sun, it is winter in the north.

Spring in the north

Summer in the north

The Sun

Why are days longer in summer?

Summer days are longer because the Earth is tilted and spins round. In summer, the Sun rises earlier and sets later. This makes daytime last longer than night. In the middle of summer in Sweden it is light for 21 hours!

Winter in
the north

Why do leaves fall in autumn?

Autumn comes between summer and winter.
Many trees lose their leaves in autumn
because it is hard for them to grow in the
dark winter months. The leaves turn from
green to red, orange or brown. Then they
fall to the ground.

Autumn in the north

Find

Can you find
photographs of red,
orange and brown
leaves in autumn?

Sunshine at midnight!

At the North and South Poles,
the Sun never sets in summer.
It is light all day. In winter,
the Sun never rises. Then it
is dark all day long!

3

What is the sunniest place?

The Sahara desert in North Africa is the sunniest place on Earth. It is sunny for nearly 12 hours every day! It hardly rains, which makes it hard for plants and animals to live here. People dress in loose clothes to prevent getting sunburnt.

Sea makes fire!

Water flowing around the sea can change the weather. El Niño is a warm water current in the Pacific Ocean. Scientists think that this could cause droughts.

When is a lake not a lake?

When it's a mirage! A mirage often happens on a hot day. Hot air near the ground makes light from the bright sky bend upwards. This makes it seem as if there is a lake on the ground in the distance. Really the ground is dry!

Remember

Can you remember why desert people wear loose clothes, even when it is very hot?

← People living in the desert

Drought ↓

What happens when it doesn't rain?

Sometimes it is dry for a long time in places where it normally rains a lot. This is called a drought. There was a drought in the United States in the 1930s. Crops didn't grow and fields turned to dust. Many people had to leave their farms.

Does Earth have a blanket?

Planet Earth

Yes, it does. The Earth is wrapped in a thick blanket of air. It is called the atmosphere. This is where all the weather happens. The atmosphere also helps to keep the Earth's surface warm at night. In the day it protects us from harmful rays coming from the Sun.

Where does it rain every day?

In a tropical rainforest the weather is always very hot and very wet. The Sun shines every day, and there are downpours of heavy rain, too. Rainforest plants grow very quickly in this steamy weather.

Monsoon downpour!

In some countries it pours with rain for a few weeks every year. This is called a monsoon. In India, enough rain falls in one year to cover the ground with water 26 metres deep!

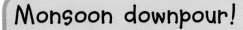

How deep is the atmosphere?

The atmosphere stretches hundreds of kilometres above our heads. If you go up through the atmosphere, the air gets thinner and thinner. High up in mountains, mountaineers find it difficult to breathe so they take breathing equipment with them.

Mountaineer

Look

Look at the picture of the Earth above. What do you think the white swirly patterns are?

7

Why does it rain?

It rains because water from oceans, rivers and lakes turns to gas in the air. If the air rises, the gas becomes water drops. These make clouds. If the drops get big enough, they fall as rain. The water then flows back to the sea.

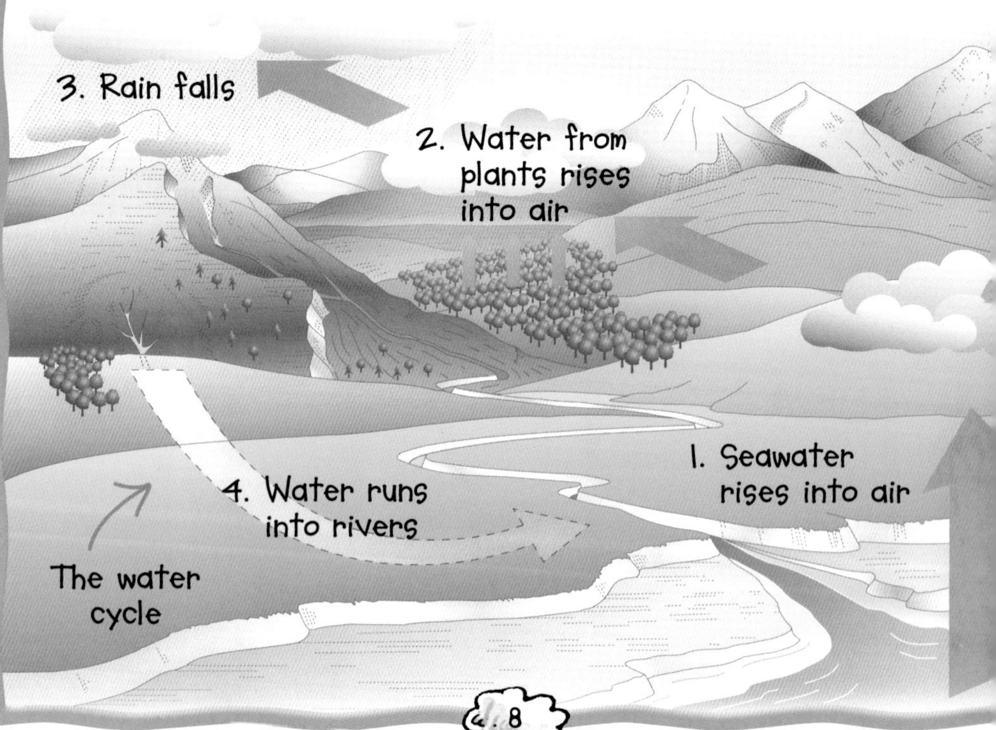

3. Rain falls

2. Water from plants rises into air

1. Seawater rises into air

4. Water runs into rivers

The water cycle

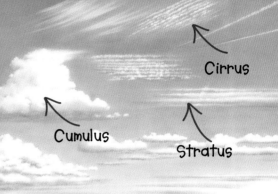

Head in the clouds!

The tops of tall mountains are often in the clouds. At the top it looks misty. Mountaineers sometimes get lost in these clouds!

Cirrus

Cumulus

Stratus

Are all clouds small and fluffy?

Clouds come in lots of different shapes and sizes. Weather experts give the different clouds names. Fluffy clouds are called cumulus clouds. Some are small and some are giant. Flat clouds are called stratus clouds. Wispy clouds high in the sky are called cirrus clouds.

What rain never lands?

Sometimes rain that falls from a cloud never reaches the ground. If the drops of rain fall into very dry air, the water in them turns into gas. This means that the drops disappear and never reach the ground.

Look

Look at the clouds outside today. Are they fluffy or flat? The picture above will help you.

What happens in a flood?

Sometimes a lot of rain falls in a few hours. So much water flows into rivers that they fill up and burst their banks. The rivers flood the land on each side. Sometimes houses disappear under the flood water.

Floods of tears!

The river Nile in Egypt floods every year. Thousands of years ago, the Egyptians made up a story about the flood. It said that a goddess called Isis cried so much that the river filled up with her tears.

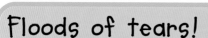

Did Noah build an ark?

The Bible tells the story of a man called Noah. He built a great boat called an ark to escape a flood. We don't know if Noah's ark existed. Scientists have found out that there probably was a huge flood thousands of years ago.

Noah's ark

Flooded house

Find

Can you find the country of Egypt and the river Nile in an atlas?

Can there be a flood in a desert?

Yes there can. Most of the time there is no rain in a desert. The hot Sun bakes the ground hard. Once in a while, it rains heavily. The water flows off the ground instead of soaking in. This can cause a flood.

What is snow made of?

Snow is made of ice, which is water that has frozen. When it is very cold in a cloud, tiny bits of ice (crystals) begin to form, instead of water drops. The pieces clump together to make snowflakes that fall to the ground. The weather must be very cold for snow to fall. If it is too warm, the snowflakes melt and turn to rain.

Shiver!

Antarctica is the coldest place on Earth. The lowest temperature ever recorded there is −89°C. That's much, much colder than inside a freezer!

Snow drifts

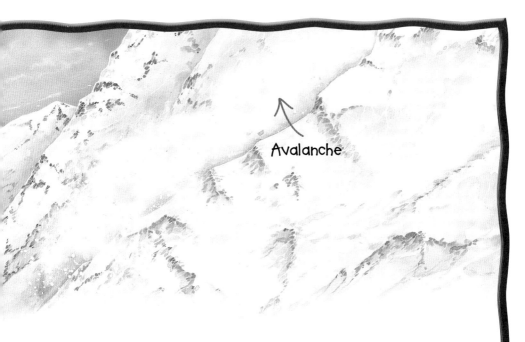

Avalanche

When is snow dangerous?

When lots of snow falls on mountains, deep layers build up on the slopes. The snow may suddenly slide down the mountain. This is an avalanche. A big avalanche can bury a town. A loud noise or even a person walking on the snow can start an avalanche.

Are all snowflakes the same?

It's hard to believe, but all snowflakes are different — even though there are millions and millions of them. This is because every ice crystal in a snowflake has its own shape. No two crystals are the same. Most ice crystals in snowflakes looks like stars with six points.

Think

Can you think why it could be dangerous to ski across a steep hillside covered with snow?

Where are the fastest winds?

Inside a tornado. A tornado is like a spinning funnel made of air. They reach down from giant thunderstorms. The winds can blow at 480 kilometres an hour. That's twice as fast as an express train! Tornadoes can rip trees from the ground and destroy houses.

Tornado

Which storm has an eye?

A hurricane is a giant spinning storm made up of super-strong winds. The centre is a hole called the eye. Here it is calm and sunny. If a hurricane reaches land, the winds can damage buildings and heavy rain causes floods. Hurricane hunters are planes that fly into hurricanes to measure the wind speed.

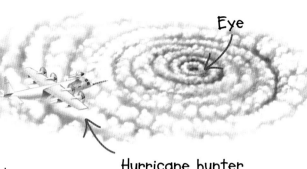

Eye

Hurricane hunter

Stormy names!

A tropical storm that starts in the Atlantic Ocean is called a hurricane. In the Pacific Ocean, a tropical storm is called a typhoon. In the Indian Ocean it is called a cyclone.

Draw

Look at the pictures on this page. Can you draw a picture of a tornado and a hurricane?

How do we measure wind?

We measure the wind on a scale called the Beaufort Scale. The slowest wind is Force 1 on the scale. This is called a light breeze. The strongest wind is Force 12. This is called a hurricane. Force zero means there is no wind at all.

What makes the sky clap?

A thunderstorm! Inside a big thundercloud, water drops and bits of ice move up and down, bumping into each other. This makes electricity build up. When the electricity jumps around, we see a spark of lightning and hear a loud clap of thunder.

Huge hail!

Hail is made up of lumps of ice called hailstones. Hail can fall from thunderclouds. The biggest hailstone ever fell in Bangladesh in 1986. It was the size of a grapefruit!

When is lightning like a fork?

When lightning jumps from a thundercloud to the ground, it looks like huge forks in the sky. If lightning jumps from one cloud to another, the clouds light up. This is called sheet lightning. Lightning can be red, blue, yellow or white.

Lightning

Does lightning hit buildings?

Lightning often hits tall buildings. The buildings have a metal spike on top called a lightning conductor. When lightning hits a building, the lightning conductor carries the electricity to the ground. If there was no lightning conductor, the building could be damaged by the lightning.

Thundercloud

Count

Count the seconds between a flash of lightning and a clap of thunder. The bigger the number, the further away the thunderstorm.

What is a rainbow made of?

Rainbow

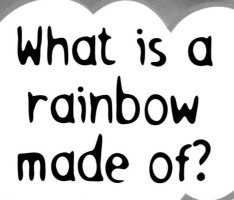

A rainbow is made of sunlight. The light bounces through raindrops. This splits the light into different colours. The colours of a rainbow are always the same. They are red, orange, yellow, green, blue, indigo and violet.

Remember

Can you remember all seven colours of a rainbow?

Northern lights

When does the sky have curtains?

In the far north and the far south of the world, amazing patterns of light sometimes appear in the sky. They look like colourful curtains. The patterns are called auroras (or-roar-rers). They happen when tiny light particles from the Sun smash into the air.

Rainbow with no colour!

A fogbow is a rainbow that is white. You might see a fogbow when the Sun shines through fog. It is white because the water drops in fog are too small to split up the light into rainbow colours.

When can you see three suns?

If there are thin clouds high in the sky, you might see three suns. The clouds are made of bits of ice. These bend light from the Sun. This makes it look as if there are two extra suns in the sky. We call these mock suns, or sun dogs.

Which bird spins in the wind?

A metal cockerel on a weather vane. The cockerel spins so it can point in any direction. When the wind blows, the cockerel spins and points to where the wind is coming from. If the wind is blowing from the north, it is called a north wind. The wind blows from the north, south, east and west.

Weather vane

Groundhog Day!

In the USA, February 2 is called Groundhog Day. If people see an animal called a groundhog, they think that it will stay cold for another six weeks!

What is a weather house?

A weather house is a model that can tell how much moisture is in the air. If it is going to be dry, a lady in summer clothes comes out. If it is going to be rainy, a man with an umbrella comes out.

Weather house

How do we know how hot it is?

By reading a thermometer. A thermometer shows the temperature, which is how hot the air around us is. The first thermometer was made in 1714 by Gabriel Daniel Fahrenheit.

Think

From which direction does a southerly wind blow? North or south?

Can planes tell the weather?

Weather planes don't carry any passengers. Instead they fly through the air recording the weather. They measure the temperature of the air, the speed of the wind and how much water is in the air. This information helps weather forecasters tell us what the weather is going to be like.

Weather plane

Astronaut snaps!

Astronauts who travel on the space shuttle and live on space stations take cameras with them. They often take amazing photographs of clouds and thunderstorms from space.

Why do scientists fly balloons?

Scientists fly balloons to find out about the weather. The balloons are filled with a gas called helium. They float up through the air and carry instruments that measure the weather. The information is sent back to the ground by radio.

Weather balloon

How do we watch weather from space?

With weather satellites. A satellite moves around the Earth in space. It takes photographs of the clouds below and sends them back to Earth. Satellite photographs show which way hurricanes are moving. They help forecasters to warn people if a hurricane is heading their way.

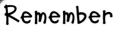

Remember

Can you remember how information gets from a weather balloon down to the ground?

23

Index

First published in 2005 by
Miles Kelly Publishing Ltd, Harding's Bar
Bardfield End Green, Thaxted, Essex,
CM6 3PX, UK

Copyright © Miles Kelly Publishing Ltd 20

This edition published 2012

2 4 6 8 10 9 7 5 3 1

Publishing Director Belinda Gallagh
Creative Director Jo Cowan
Managing Editor Amanda Askew
Volume Designer Sophie Pelham
Cover Designer Jo Cowan
Indexer Helen Snaith
Production Manager Elizabeth Colli
Reprographics Stephan Davis,
Lorraine King
Character Cartoonist Mike Foster

ISBN 978-1-84810-898-1

Printed in China

British Library Cataloguing-in-Publication D
A catalogue record for this book is availc
from the British Library

ACKNOWLEDGEMENTS
All artwork from the Miles Kelly Artwork Bo
The publishers would like to thank
Alexander Maier/fotolia.com for the use
the cover photograph
All other photographs are from:
Corel, digitalSTOCK, digitalvision, John Fo
PhotoAlto, PhotoDisc, PhotoEssentials, Photo
Stockbyte
Every effort has been made to acknowledge
source and copyright holder of each pictur
Miles Kelly Publishing apologises for any
unintentional errors or omissions.
Made with paper from a sustainable forest

www.mileskelly.net
info@mileskelly.net

www.factsforprojects.com